THE TRUTH IS

1. Leveling up your craft to write a story that lives long after you've left the planet is what some might call a ridiculous goal.

2. You will not tell that story after reading just one how-to-write book.

3. You will not tell that story as the result of taking one seminar.

4. You know creating a timeless work of art will require the dedication of a world-class athlete. You will be training your mind with as much ferocity and single-minded purpose as an Olympic gold medal hopeful. That kind of cognitive regimen excites you, but you just haven't found a convincing storytelling dojo to do that work.

5. The path to leveling up your creative craft is a dark and treacherous one. You've been at it a long time, and it often feels like you're wearing three-dimensional horse blinders. More times than you'd like to admit, you're not sure if you're moving north or south or east or west. And the worst part? You can't see anyone else, anywhere, going through what you're going through. You're all alone.

WELCOME TO THE STORY GRID UNIVERSE

1. We believe we find meaning in the pursuit of creations that last longer than we do. This is *not* ridiculous. Seizing opportunities and overcoming obstacles as we stretch ourselves to reach for seemingly unreachable creations is transformational. We believe this pursuit is the most valuable and honorable way to spend our time here. Even if—especially if—we never reach our lofty creative goals.

2. Writing just one story isn't going to take us to the top. We're moving from point A to Point A^{5000}. We've got lots of mountains to climb, lots of rivers and oceans to cross, and many deep dark forests to traverse along the way. We need topographic guides, and if they're not available, we'll have to figure out how to write them ourselves.

3. We're drawn to seminars to consume the imparted wisdom of an icon in the arena, but we leave with something far more valuable than the curriculum. We get to meet the universe's other pilgrims and compare notes on the terrain.

4. The Story Grid Universe has a virtual dojo, a university in which to work out and get stronger—a place to stumble, correct mistakes, and stumble again, until the moves become automatic and mesmerizing to outside observers.

5. The Story Grid Universe has a performance space, a publishing house dedicated to leveling up the craft with clear boundaries of progress and the ancillary reference resources to pack for each project mission. There are an infinite number of paths to where you want to be, with a story that works. Seeing how others have made it down their own yellow-brick roads to release their creations into the timeless creative cosmos will help keep you on the straight and narrow path.

All are welcome—the more, the merrier. But please abide by the golden rule:

Put the work above all else, and trust the process.

THE FIVE COMMANDMENTS OF STORYTELLING

DANIELLE KIOWSKI

STORY GRID

STORY GRID

Story Grid Publishing LLC
223 Egremont Plain Road
PMB 191
Egremont, MA 01230

First Story Grid Publishing Paperback Edition
October 2021

For Information about Special Discounts for Bulk
Purchases,
Please visit www.storygridpublishing.com

ISBN: 978-1-64501-077-7
Ebook: 978-1-64501-078-4

For

All Past, Present, and Future Story Nerds

ABOUT THIS BOOK

Think about the experience you want your story to create for your readers. Do you want your readers to immerse themselves in your story? Do you want to shatter worldviews and change lives? Do you want to give them an entertaining read that keeps them turning pages?

Before you can accomplish any of these goals, you need to understand the foundational principles of Story. To help you understand the fundamental structure of Story, this book explores five core components you will find in every story that works, across every medium. Epic fantasy tomes have them. Page-turning thrillers have them. Literary masterpieces have them. Even a knock-knock joke has them.

These are the Five Commandments of Storytelling. You need them to engage your audience in your story. You need them for any kind of story that works.

As writers, we want to tell stories that work to make a lasting impact on our audience.

In this book, you'll learn how to build a story that does just that by crafting five critical components that work together to create a cohesive and compelling arc. The tools are based on psychological research and the analysis of stories that have stood the test of time. The skills you'll learn give you what you need to tell a story that will matter to your reader.

Whatever level of experience and skill you have with storytelling or the Story Grid methodology, this is an opportunity to deepen your understanding of the foundational principles of Story. When you invest in strengthening your understanding of the fundamentals of Story, the impacts resonate throughout your work to make your writing more effective and impactful.

1

WHY WE TELL STORIES

We create stories to communicate with an audience. As artists, we have something to say, and our stories are the way we pass that message on to audiences that we'll never meet, across space and time.

When we set out to communicate a message that matters, we have many choices for getting it across to our intended audience. Messages surround us every day. Consider the example of the message that we should be thankful for what we have. We see this repeated all the time in news articles, radio segments, and posted signs—like the signs at restaurants saying, "We don't have wi-fi. Talk to each other." We could read academic papers detailing studies that show the power of gratitude. People in our lives might repeat adages, telling us to stop and smell the roses. If we're acting in a harmful way, well-meaning relatives and friends might tell us directly that we need to change what we're doing. All of us have heard this message thousands of times. I know I have. Still, every time I see *It's a Wonderful Life*, I am glued to the screen as George Bailey discovers this truth for himself, and I cry when he finally reunites with his family and sees the value of the gifts in his life. For many people, watching this story unfold is a yearly tradition. Why does it stick with us?

Narrative is a powerful medium because it bypasses the audience's resistance and delivers a message they would ordinarily block out. For thousands of years, people have understood the impact a well-crafted story has on the audience.

One of Aesop's fables, "The North Wind and the Sun," shows us how this works. One day, the wind and sun had an argument about which was stronger. The two spotted a traveler on the road and agreed that the one that could get him to remove his coat would be the stronger. The wind tried to blow the coat off the traveler's back, but he only wrapped it tighter and hunkered down against the gale. Then, it was the sun's turn to try. The sun shone its rays down on the traveler, heating him up. Soon, the traveler removed the coat.

The sun accomplished the desired effect with minimum effort because the traveler thought removing the coat was his own idea.

Persuasion works best when you convince the audience they've decided to change on their own. That's the power of story. Aesop knew that. After all, he told his fables in story form to carry his messages to audiences.

Stories communicate a subtle message to an audience, just as the sun gradually warms the traveler in the fable. Instead of shining, the author creates avatars, which simulate human beings, to act out the story. Without even realizing it, the audience starts to care about them. They connect with the protagonist and accompany them on their journey, watching them grow and change throughout the story. Along the way, audience members change, too.

The audience experiences the story and learns the core message on their own. Through the magic of story, the audience connects with avatars that seem completely different from them. However, they learn that underneath different exteriors, the human experience is universal. In this way, stories bind us together to overcome prejudices and change the world.

This is why learning the craft of storytelling is so important. Well-crafted stories can capture audiences and deliver compelling ideas, but poorly told stories drive audiences away. To tell your story well, you need to know what makes a story work.

2

THE FIVE COMMANDMENTS OF STORYTELLING

Every effective story has five critical components that work together to communicate a message in a way that bypasses readers' critical minds to touch their hearts and change their worldviews. These components are the Five Commandments of Storytelling.

The Five Commandments ensure that your story resonates with your readers to communicate the message you want to convey. The Five Commandments accomplish this because they simulate psychological patterns that people use to solve problems and process change, and they follow patterns found in stories that have stood the test of time. The Five Commandments work.

The message they communicate to the reader is called the controlling idea. This is a statement of the central lesson of the story—

the idea the reader will take away from the story and integrate into how they see the world.

The controlling idea is made up of the story's value shift and the protagonist's action. Let's examine how each piece of this statement contributes to the message the story conveys to the reader.

A value shift signals the global genre of the story. Each genre has a core value spectrum that stories within that genre explore. The controlling idea focuses on the value state at the end of the story. A Love story's controlling idea might begin with *Love triumphs...* or *Hate results...* while a Crime story might be *Justice prevails...* or *Tyranny reigns...* This shows the reader the impact of using this story as a pattern for behavior.

The other half of the controlling idea describes the protagonist's action. In this book, you'll learn to recognize the moment in the story that matters most to the controlling idea and how to evaluate the protagonist's choice to create a succinct statement of the pivotal action.

The value shift and the protagonist's action come together to form one sentence that encapsulates the lesson and drives your story —your controlling idea.

The Five Commandments of Storytelling

are the signposts that mark the journey you take with the reader as you communicate your controlling idea. They are a form, not a formula. This means they have universal characteristics that make them effective in any story, but your commandments will be unique to the specific world of your story.

In the following sections, I'll walk you through each of the Five Commandments in detail. You'll learn:

- How the commandment functions in your story.
- How it contributes to your controlling idea.
- Why it matters to your reader.
- What to consider when constructing the commandment in your own story.

I'll show you how the Five Commandments function in different units of story. Global stories are made up of quadrants, sequences, scenes, and beats. Each unit must include the Five Commandments, and the commandments within each unit help it to function effectively individually and as part of the whole.

In the individual commandment sections, I'll focus on the universal characteristics of each commandment, using examples from global stories. However, keep in mind that the same considerations apply when constructing the Five Commandments for smaller units. We'll go over how to do that once you have a foundational understanding of how to build each commandment.

Finally, I'll go over how the Five Commandments work together to create a compelling story and convey the message you want to communicate to your reader.

3

COMMANDMENT ONE: THE INCITING INCIDENT

The inciting incident is a ball of chaos that spins into the story and knocks the protagonist's life out of balance. It puts the events of the story into motion and introduces the reader to the global conflict in a compelling way.

Your inciting incident sets up the rest of your story. It establishes the arena in which the controlling idea operates. It grounds reader expectations for a satisfying experience while drawing your audience into the flow of the narrative.

DEFINING THE INCITING INCIDENT

To kick off events in a way that interests your reader and creates the right expectations for the rest of the story, you'll need an event with the necessary characteristics to function as an inciting incident. Let's go over what makes an inciting incident work.

An effective inciting incident is an **invisible phere gorilla** that **interrupts the protagonist's status quo.**

Invisible Phere Gorilla

The term "invisible phere gorilla" is a combination of two terms: *phere* and *invisible gorilla*. We'll examine both components individually and then explore how they come together to form one concept.

A phere is a moment of unexpected change and challenge. The phere, as a representation of the chaotic nature of the universe, contains within it the potential for destruction and creation. Both forces swirl within it until an agent can metabolize the phere and realize its potential.

An invisible gorilla is something that exists in plain sight, but the mind filters it out of our perception. This might sound incredible— after all, we like to think we can see what's right in front of us. However, this happens all the time. Christopher Chabris and Daniel Simons conducted an experiment that showed the power of inattentional blindness, or the masking capability of the human mind. In this experiment, subjects observed people on a basketball court and counted how many passes they made. In the middle of the counting time period, a person in a gorilla suit walked through the court. Half of the subjects blocked out the gorilla from their conscious perception and didn't see it at all. This capacity to filter our perception saves us from a barrage of sensory input, allowing us to focus on what matters, but we risk missing something important.

The invisible phere gorilla combines these terms into one concept. The phere, with all its potential energy, sits inside an invisible gorilla. The gorilla is a disguise that enshrouds the phere and hides its true nature from the protagonist. Over the course of the story, the protagonist must learn to see the truth of the invisible phere gorilla to metabolize the unexpected change of the phere.

Interruption of the Status Quo

Not all inciting incidents are suited to all protagonists. The invisible phere gorilla acts as a magnet, attracting the right protagonist to respond to the event—the one that needs to metabolize the particular kind of unexpected change the inciting incident offers. The phere drops in and upsets the balance of the protagonist's life, prompting them into action to resolve the imbalance. At the same time, the invisible gorilla challenges the unconscious cognitive frame that limits the protagonist—the limited perspective the protagonist must break in order to grow. To process the phere, the protagonist has to break through its invisible gorilla disguise by confronting the unconscious filters that have allowed it to remain invisible.

The invisible phere gorilla must cause imbalance in the protagonist's life, interrupting the status quo and forcing change. It must directly affect the protagonist, so if the inciting incident remains unresolved, the protagonist will suffer consequences.

The imbalance, and the necessity of response, creates or crystallizes the object of desire for the protagonist. If the inciting incident introduces a new imbalance, it creates a desire in the protagonist. For example, if someone commits a crime, the goal of solving that crime arises. In other cases, an existing desire finds focus in the inciting incident. The protagonist of a Love story has an existing need for love, and the inciting incident presents the potential partner as a candidate for fulfillment of that need. The external imbalance creates a want for the protagonist while the invisible gorilla's challenge to the cognitive frame creates a need for change.

When the reader sees the protagonist

pursue a goal, it evokes empathy and helps the reader immerse in the story. The creation of the object of desire also generates narrative drive because it poses a question about how the protagonist will process the phere to achieve the goal. The setup implicitly promises that the story will provide the answer to the question, and it establishes how the character must change to solve the problem. The audience is hooked and keeps reading to see how the story fulfills its promise.

BUILDING THE INCITING INCIDENT

As you construct a story event with the universal characteristics of an effective inciting incident, consider its category and placement to ensure your inciting incident fits the specific needs of your story.

Categories

All inciting incidents fall into two categories: causal and coincidental.

A **causal** inciting incident happens as a direct result of a choice made by someone in the story. For example, in *The Silence of the Lambs*, Jack Crawford sets the story into motion by selecting Clarice Starling to interview Hannibal Lecter. This is a conscious choice to involve Starling in the investigation.

The responsible agent doesn't need to understand the consequences of the causal inciting incident. In *Pride and Prejudice*, Bingley moves to Netherfield with no intention of serving as the inciting incident for a Love story, but he attracts the interest of the Bennets nevertheless. This is still a causal inciting incident because the consequences arise from his choice.

Coincidental inciting incidents arise out of random, chaotic chance. They are not the result of anyone's actions. The cyclone in *The Wonderful Wizard of Oz* and the storm in *The Martian* are examples of this category, but coincidental inciting incidents can be more than just weather patterns. They also include accidents, deaths by natural causes, and chance encounters.

Some inciting incidents seem to fall into a third category between causal and coincidental. They are **ambiguous**, which means the reader can't tell whether an agent caused the event or not. In *The Hound of the Baskervilles*, the inciting incident of the global story is the murder of Sir Charles Baskerville. In the initial investigation, it seems that Sir Charles died of natural causes. He had a history of heart problems and died of a heart attack. However, his friend Dr. James Mortimer thinks a sinister family curse was the real cause of Sir Charles's death, and he hires Sherlock Holmes to find the truth. Holmes discovers that Sir Charles was murdered, and the method of murder is part of the mystery. An ambiguous inciting incident like this one can intrigue the reader, but by the end of the story the reader must know if it was a causal or coincidental event. The discovery of the true nature of the inciting incident is part of the protagonist's metabolization of the unexpected change.

Placement

Your inciting incident should happen at or near the beginning of the unit of story, but its exact placement depends on the requirements of the narrative. Inciting incidents may be immediate, delayed, or off-page.

An **immediate** inciting incident happens at the beginning of the unit of story. This immerses the reader in the global story right away. The drawback is that the reader must acclimate to the world while they process the inciting incident. This option is best suited to stories with primal stakes. Examples include the discovery of a body or getting trapped in a storm. The reader connects with the protagonist when they see these universally relevant events.

Delayed inciting incidents still happen near the beginning, but they occur after events that set up the unit of story. At the global level, the inciting incident may be several scenes into the work. This choice allows for introduction of the stakes and the world before the inciting incident. The tradeoff is that the global story does not start immediately. With this option, it's important to build conflict into the setup scenes to keep the reader's attention. Delaying the inciting incident is a good choice for events that need more explanation for the reader to connect with the protagonist in the way the author intends. For example, in the inciting incident of *Gone Girl*, Nick's wife disappears. This is a primal inciting incident that would normally inspire empathy for Nick, but the setup scenes lead the reader to suspect Nick instead of fully identifying with him.

If the inciting incident happens **off-page** before the unit of story begins, the story begins *in medias res*. This Latin phrase means "in the middle of things." It plunges the reader into the action. The reader is immediately immersed in the story, but they must do more work to figure out what happened before the narrative started. This is the best option when the protagonist must discover something about the inciting incident. For example, in *The Hound of the Baskervilles*, the crime happens off-page because Sherlock Holmes must investigate whether Sir Charles was actually murdered. Crime stories often start this way.

Keep these considerations in mind when you build an inciting incident for your story so you can create an event that fulfills the universal requirements of the inciting incident and also works well with your specific story.

ANALYZING THE INCITING INCIDENT

When you study a story example or review your own writing, use the following list of questions to verify that the inciting incident has the characteristics it needs to function effectively.

- **Causal or Coincidental?** Identify the category of the inciting incident. Remember that even if it's not clear when the inciting incident happens, by the end of the story the reader must be able to place the event in one of the categories.
- **How does it create imbalance?** The inciting incident must directly impact the protagonist, and there must be consequences if the

protagonist fails to respond. Determine how the protagonist's life is knocked off-balance and what the impact of ignoring the event would be.

- **What does it promise?** Look at the question raised by the inciting incident to describe the kind of answer it promises to the reader. Keep this in mind as you build out the rest of the Five Commandments.
- **How is it invisible?** There must be something about the inciting incident that the protagonist does not understand. Determine what misinterpretation operates at the beginning of the story.

An effective inciting incident is causal or coincidental, disturbs the balance of the protagonist's life, promises a compelling climax, and is disguised as an invisible gorilla. An event with these characteristics sets up your story in a compelling way. It promises consequences and challenges your protagonist's established cognitive frame, generating a want and need that define the landscape in which your controlling idea operates. This primes your reader to receive the message you want to communicate with your story.

In response to the inciting incident, the protagonist develops a strategy to correct the imbalance and get back to the status quo, but they still operate under the established cognitive frame until the strategy fails when the protagonist reaches the turning point progressive complication (Commandment Two).

4

COMMANDMENT TWO: THE TURNING POINT PROGRESSIVE COMPLICATION

The turning point progressive complication marks the point at which the protagonist's initial strategy for responding to the inciting incident fails. It shows that the protagonist's established cognitive frame, or limited perspective, is not sufficient to deal with the problem posed by the inciting incident.

This is a compelling moment because the inciting incident created an empathetic link between the reader and the protagonist, who must now change in some way. The reader experiences the turning point along with the protagonist.

DEFINING THE TURNING POINT PROGRESSIVE COMPLICATION

The turning point progressive complication is an event that falls into the broader category of progressive complications. To understand the turning point progressive complication, let's explore the definition of a progressive complication and the special case of one that functions as a turning point.

Progressive Complications

A complication is an unexpected event. The protagonist of a story chooses how to act with the expectation that things will work out in a certain way. An expected response to an action is boring. When we, or the avatars we observe in a story, get what we expected, we are not challenged to change. Everything is in balance. It gives us comfort but not growth. We aren't forced to change, so we don't. If nothing changes, it's not a story.

Stories are all about change, so the unexpected event is the lifeblood of a story. Complications are (or should be) happening all the time. They can be large or small and positive or negative—but they must be unexpected.

For the narrative to make sense, complications must not only be present, but they must be directed in a way that forces the protagonist to grapple with the problem at the heart of the story. Complications that funnel the protagonist toward a moment of confrontation with the invisible phere gorilla are **progressive complications**. If complications are progressive, each successive complication presents an increased challenge to the protagonist because it becomes harder and harder to go back.

Complications must also be relevant to the story. A complication is relevant if it relates to the protagonist's journey to obtain the object of desire. This means it affects the protagonist's strategy to pursue the want that arose in the inciting incident.

An effective series of relevant progressive complications creates a narrative arc that forces the protagonist toward meaningful change by cutting off alternative options to obtain the objects of desire. As the protagonist acts in pursuit of the goal, their tactics prove useless, and they get back unexpected results. They cling to any remaining skills they have in their familiar toolkit until, finally, they are forced to confront the truth that their habitual cognitive frame is not equipped to handle the problem they face.

Note that progressive complications happen in every unit of story, so we will see complications within the scenes or beats of the other commandments. To identify the complication that's the most relevant for the Five Commandments analysis, we'll need to determine which progressive complication is the turning point.

Turning Point

The **turning point** is the progressive complication that shows the protagonist that their habitual strategy will not work to solve the problem presented by the inciting incident. This moment illustrates that their tactics are failing because of a larger problem. Their strategy is not suited to the situation at hand. It shines a spotlight on the invisible phere gorilla, revealing its true nature and, at the same time, exposing the elements of the protagonist's cognitive frame that have allowed it to remain invisible.

The protagonist can't go on as before. After the turning point, continuing with the original strategy is either impossible or has new consequences for the protagonist. For example, in *The Wonderful Wizard of Oz*, Dorothy follows the strategy of trusting Oz to get her back home. However, when she and her companions discover that Oz is a fraud, she can no longer rely on the power of the wizard for help. Following her original strategy is impossible. In *The Hound of the Baskervilles*, Sherlock Holmes's strategy is to watch events unfold from his hiding place on the moor. The turning point is when the murderer attempts to kill Sir Henry and accidentally kills Selden, a convict living on the moor, instead. Holmes is forced to reconsider his strategy. It is still possible for him to watch from the moor, but Selden's death has increased the stakes of this choice. Holmes understands that Sir Henry Baskerville's life is in danger, so if he continues with his original strategy, he must now face new consequences.

When the protagonist faces the impossibility of staying the same, they are forced to change. The turning point creates a direct chain of events that will show how the protagonist changes or fails to change, which ultimately shifts the value of the unit of story. As the first link in this chain, the turning point exposes the change that will be necessary for the protagonist to accomplish the value shift.

BUILDING THE TURNING POINT PROGRESSIVE COMPLICATION

When you create a turning point progressive complication, you can choose the category of turning point that fits best in the unit of story. You can also determine whether a positive or negative turning point serves the story.

Categories

Turning points may be active or revelatory.

Active turning points are complications that arise because of characters' actions. Someone does something that renders the protagonist's initial strategy useless. The agent responsible for the action does not need to intend the consequences of the action. The effect on the protagonist, not the motivation of the action, matters for the turning point. In *The Hound of the Baskervilles*, Selden dies because Stapleton has released the hound in an attempt to kill Sir Henry. This is an active turning point because Stapleton's murder attempt is an action.

Revelatory turning points offer new information that forces the protagonist to change. An example of this is the turning point of *The Wonderful Wizard of Oz*. When Dorothy and her friends discover that Oz is a fraud, the new information shatters their reliance on the wizard for help getting what they need and returning Dorothy to Kansas.

In practice, the distinction between active and revelatory turning points is not always clear. An action can reveal information, and the discovery of information can inspire actions. For example, in *Pride and Prejudice*, Darcy's proposal to Elizabeth is an action that reveals his feelings for her. To categorize this kind of turning point, determine whether any new information is created in the event. When Dorothy and her friends discover Oz's deception, they uncover information that existed long before they came to the Emerald City. Their discovery does not alter the underlying facts. On the other hand, when Darcy proposes, the dynamic shifts in Elizabeth and Darcy's relationship. His action creates new information beyond the revelation of his attraction that existed before his proposal. Because of this, it's an active turning point.

Both categories of turning points can be powerful. Use big revelations sparingly to avoid losing your audience—but if the moment is right, they can have a profound impact. Which you choose depends on the kind of invisibility you've created in your inciting incident. Consider which category of complication will best expose the true nature of the invisible phere gorilla.

Valence

Progressive complications and, more specifically, turning points may be either negative or positive events. Each complication is an obstacle or an affordance on the journey to obtain the protagonist's objects of desire.

An **obstacle** is a negative event that blocks the protagonist's pursuit of the goal. The failure of a tactic based in the protagonist's original cognitive frame exposes the underlying failure of the strategy. In *The Wonderful Wizard of Oz*, discovering that Oz is a fraud seems to destroy all hope that Dorothy will get home.

A positive event is an **affordance**. In this case, getting what the protagonist wants exposes the need to change. With an apparent success, the protagonist seems to get what they want—but that achievement is unsatisfying without the accompanying worldview shift. When Darcy proposes, it seems that Elizabeth has made a good match and saved herself from the destitution she faces from the entailment of her family estate. However, to accept the proposal, she would have to deny her authentic self. The opportunity for success shows Elizabeth what she truly needs.

To find the best fit for your story, consider whether an apparent loss or win is the most effective way to shatter your protagonist's existing worldview.

ANALYZING THE TURNING POINT PROGRESSIVE COMPLICATION

The following questions will help you determine whether a turning point—either in your own work or in a story example you're studying—has what it needs to create a shift in the story.

- **Active or Revelatory?** Determine the category of the turning point. If you get stuck, analyze whether the turning point event creates new information for the protagonist to process or exposes existing information.
- **What is the protagonist's initial strategy?** Identify the strategy the protagonist follows in response to the inciting incident. Find the common thread that unites the tactics the protagonist employs in the first part of the story to understand the worldview at play in the protagonist's actions.
- **How does this moment make that impossible?** Effective turning points make the protagonist switch gears. To answer this question, identify how the turning point stops the

protagonist from pursuing their original strategy or, if it is still possible, how the turning point has created new consequences for following the same path.

The turning point is a powerful moment for the audience. The reader—who empathizes with the protagonist as a result of the objects of desire that arise in the inciting incident—experiences the failure of the established worldview along with the protagonist. When the turning point exposes the change necessary for the protagonist to accomplish the value shift, the reader faces the choice of whether to change, too. They reflect on the limitations in their own cognitive frame as the invisible phere gorilla's true nature is exposed.

Once the protagonist—and the reader—realize the limitations of their worldview, they must make a choice about what to do with that information. The choice they face is the third commandment, the crisis.

5

COMMANDMENT THREE: THE CRISIS

The crisis is the dilemma that the protagonist faces as a result of the turning point. It's a choice between incompatible options. The protagonist can't have everything.

Developing the crisis outlines the choices the protagonist recognizes in the face of the turning point and defines what's at stake. The reader makes an emotional investment in the stakes, so the crisis increases narrative drive and propels the reader into the rest of the story.

DEFINING THE CRISIS

The crisis arises out of the turning point. Once the protagonist can no longer pursue the initial strategy, they must choose how, or whether, to continue the pursuit of the object of desire. At the core, the crisis is about whether to break the original cognitive frame and develop a new worldview or to double down on their existing worldview and try new tactics to make the extraordinary world adapt to their existing frame.

To develop a crisis choice that makes the reader care about the protagonist's decision, you need to build out a compelling choice with stakes that have a real impact on the protagonist.

The crisis poses a real choice between **incompatible options** with **meaningful stakes**.

Incompatible Options

The options available to the protagonist must be mutually exclusive. This means the protagonist can't choose to pursue multiple options. Incompatible options force the protagonist to choose one strategy to move forward. No matter what they choose, they must give something up or incur a cost.

When the protagonist must choose one path, it forces them to reveal their true character. We learn about them by observing which values they prioritize over others and which costs are justified to achieve an outcome. The protagonist can say they value something, but the true test is whether they will stand by that value when they must pay a price. In *The Hound of the Baskervilles*, Sherlock Holmes values justice. As a master detective, he is a symbolic representation of the value. His commitment to justice is tested when he faces the choice of whether to put his friend's life in danger to catch a murderer. This decision allows the reader to see how much Holmes is willing to risk to pursue justice.

Meaningful Stakes

The crisis can only show the character of the protagonist if the options available have real, meaningful stakes. If the crisis has trivial stakes, the decision doesn't matter—for the narrative or the character. It's not exciting to the reader.

They might see that the protagonist's decision doesn't matter, which diminishes the narrative drive because readers are no longer invested in the outcome.

If the stakes are unbalanced, the reader will identify the obvious choice that is clearly the best option. In these cases, if the protagonist chooses the obvious option, the reader learns nothing about the character. If the protagonist chooses another option, the reader will abandon the empathic bond they've created with the avatar because they no longer seem believable or deserving of the reader's emotional investment. Either way, you risk losing your reader if you don't create meaningful stakes.

Consider whether the stakes are appropriate for the point in the story. Part of progressively complicating the story is to increase stakes over time so the challenges facing your protagonist become incrementally harder. As the stakes climb, the decisions get more difficult but also more revealing. The protagonist's true nature comes out when they are faced with seemingly impossible choices.

BUILDING THE CRISIS

As you construct the crisis, you can decide which category of choice your protagonist must face, what kind of a calculation they must make, and how you will show the stakes of the different options that are available.

Categories

Every crisis is either a best bad choice or an irreconcilable goods choice.

A **best bad choice** crisis has negative options. No matter what the protagonist chooses, there will be a cost. This type of crisis illustrates what the protagonist is willing to endure to get their desired outcome. A best bad choice crisis increases narrative drive because the reader feels anxiety about the risks the protagonist faces when they emerge from the crisis and take a course of action. For example, when Holmes considers his options in *The Hound of the Baskervilles*, we see how much harm he is willing to risk to get justice for Sir Charles's murder. On both sides, there is potential for loss. If he alerts Stapleton to his suspicions, the murderer may escape and kill again. On the other hand, if he uses Sir Henry as bait, he risks his friend's life. No matter what he chooses, the reader feels anxious heading into the rest of the story because potential disaster looms.

An **irreconcilable goods** crisis is a choice between options that offer incompatible positive outcomes. However, the protagonist can only pursue one of them. This type of crisis is often a choice between what is good for the self and good for the whole. In this situation, the protagonist must decide whether to save themselves or sacrifice to save others. It could also be a choice between pursuing a want and pursuing a need. For example, in *Pride and Prejudice*, Elizabeth must choose between remaining comfortable in her own prejudice and acknowledging the truth. She cannot have both things because facing the truth means shattering her image of her family and herself.

In both categories of crisis, each option has potential costs and benefits. The type of crisis depends on how you choose to present the options and frame the protagonist's choice. Use the categorization as a tool to help you keep the options balanced so your protagonist faces a real choice with meaningful stakes and no obvious right answer.

Problem Space

The protagonist makes a calculation in the crisis to solve the problem that the turning point presents. The method the protagonist uses depends on the type of problem they are trying to solve. The protagonist can make a prioritization or an optimization calculation. Each has a different function in the revelation of character.

In a **prioritization** crisis, the protagonist's options represent two different values. The protagonist must decide which value is more important to them. Elizabeth's choice is between the comfort of her family and established worldview, which represent safety, and personal growth, which represents truth and the potential of love with Darcy. When we consider whether safety or truth is more important, there is no obvious choice. Different characters prioritize different values, and the same person may prioritize different values in different contexts. When we see the protagonist make these kinds of choices, we learn how to make choices about how to navigate a complex interplay of values.

An **optimization** crisis is about how the protagonist makes a calculation within one value space. In this case, all of the options work within the same value, so we see how the protagonist predicts outcomes and calculates the net effect on the value they want to pursue. This is what Holmes does in *The Hound of the Baskervilles*. Both options available to him are about justice. The question he must answer is whether the risk of a murderer on the loose is worse than the risk to an innocent man serving as bait in a trap. When the protagonist makes these calculations, we can check our own predictive processing capabilities along with them.

You can show both kinds of calculations over the course of a story to explore the global value—when it should be prioritized over other values and how to calculate expected outcomes of the value. Which you emphasize depends on the message you want to convey to the reader.

Dramatization

The reader needs to see the stakes of each option available in the crisis in order to understand the risks and potential payoffs for the protagonist. They also need to see what the available options are so they understand the full landscape of the choice. Different protagonists will see different options when faced with the same problem, so it's critical to establish the possible paths. This allows the reader to see what the protagonist is not doing, which is as important as what they are doing.

You need to show the full set of options and the stakes associated with each, but you can choose when and how to impart this information to the reader.

An **internally dramatized** crisis shows the protagonist's thoughts as they go through their options. This can appear differently, depending on the narrative device. The reader might see the thoughts of the protagonist directly. If the narrative device does not permit this level of transparency, the protagonist might have a conversation with another avatar about the crisis choice. For example, in *The Wonderful Wizard of Oz*, Dorothy and her friends discuss her options in the throne room after Oz's departure. The narrator can also outline the choice in exposition. Dramatizing a crisis in this way makes the options and stakes very clear, but you risk losing the audience if you spend time giving them information they find obvious or that interrupts active moments.

If the crisis is **externally dramatized**, the author does not show the stakes of the crisis while the protagonist is processing it. In these cases, it might look like the crisis is off the page, but it's not, really. Instead, you can find clues to how the protagonist processes the crisis in other parts of the story. Look for situations where another avatar makes a similar choice to the one the protagonist is facing. Identify the consequences of their choices. When your protagonist encounters a choice like that one, the decision shown in the previous situation informs the protagonist and the reader of the available options, and the stakes are defined by the outcome that was realized in the other scene. This kind of dramatization is more subtle and requires more of the reader, but it is powerful because it gives the reader a cascade of insights as they connect the protagonist's choice to other parts of the story. This choice also shows the development of the protagonist with a full exploration of the options in the crisis but avoids interrupting narrative drive with an explanation of the protagonist's processing.

ANALYZING THE CRISIS

As you review the crisis in your draft or in a story example, answer these questions to verify that the crisis is a compelling choice that will pose a difficult dilemma for the protagonist and keep the reader engaged.

- **Best Bad Choice or Irreconcilable Goods?** Determine how the crisis is defined. Explain whether it is a choice between bad options or good options. Does it force the protagonist to accept negative consequences? Or do they need to decide between something that is good for the self and something that is good for the whole?
- **What are the protagonist's options?** Outline the options the protagonist has. Look for specific text that tells you the different options the protagonist recognizes in the situation. Ensure the protagonist can choose only one of the options.
- **What is at stake?** Explain the stakes for each option that is available in the crisis. Delineate the cost, benefit, and risk for each course of

action. This will illustrate the problem space the protagonist navigates as they consider the crisis choice.

The crisis builds narrative drive by getting the reader invested in the choice the protagonist faces. It establishes the stakes of the story, showing the cost the protagonist must pay to achieve the object of desire. The reader decides along with the protagonist whether the resulting value shift is worth the sacrifice the crisis demands.

Once the protagonist has considered the options available in the crisis—and their accompanying stakes—they must determine which action to take. This decision is the climax, the fourth commandment.

6

COMMANDMENT FOUR: THE CLIMAX

The climax shows the protagonist's decision when they choose one of the options outlined in the crisis or come up with an alternative option they didn't recognize before. The protagonist not only makes the decision but actualizes the decision by taking action. This allows the reader to see the impact of the decision in the world of the story.

This high-energy moment rewards the reader's emotional investment in the story. The climax fulfills the promise of the inciting incident, satisfying the reader's expectations while providing a surprising and unexpected story event.

DEFINING THE CLIMAX

The climax is the event the reader has been waiting for. It answers the question posed by the inciting incident. The invisible phere gorilla's true nature is clear, and the protagonist shows how they choose to deal with it by taking action.

In the climax, the protagonist enacts the decision they make after considering the dilemma in the crisis. When the audience sees what they have chosen to do, this reveals information about the protagonist's character. The reader identified the options and stakes available to the protagonist during the crisis, so when they see the protagonist's choice, they understand the required sacrifice. They can see what the protagonist chooses to prioritize and what they are willing to give up.

The climax both illustrates and proves the changes the character has gone through. This action shows the protagonist acting in a way they were not capable of at the beginning of the story. To showcase the change, the climax mirrors the inciting incident. The change the protagonist has gone through enables them to respond to situations that used to be invisible to them because of their cognitive frame.

Before the climax, the protagonist may commit to a plan of action or communicate the change they have undergone. However, the protagonist's change is just potential until they realize it by taking action in the climax. For example, in *Pride and Prejudice*, Elizabeth takes

Darcy's letter to heart and abandons her prejudices. She begins to display evidence of her changed cognitive frame by warning her father about Lydia and Wickham. However, she must fully commit to her choice. In the climax, Elizabeth confesses her feelings to Darcy. She risks humiliation to actualize her changed worldview.

The climax is an important moment because it provides proof of the shift in cognitive framing that will act as the catalyst for the value change in the controlling idea. This proof is required to show that real transformation drives the value shift in the controlling idea.

BUILDING THE CLIMAX

When you create a climax for your story, consider the active character and the complications of the event to ensure you are building an effective story event and avoiding common problems with the climax.

Deus Ex Machina

The protagonist must make the choice in the climax. A common problem with climactic actions is deus ex machina. This phrase dates from early Greek theater, when playwrights would resolve impossible situations by using a rig to fly an actor, playing a god or goddess, over the stage. The deity would use supernatural powers to resolve the situation in favor of the protagonist. Deus ex machina means "god in the machine," and refers to the contraptions the actors used to fly.

In the modern equivalent, another avatar intervenes and makes the choice or carries out the climactic action for the protagonist. This undermines the investment the reader has made in empathizing with the protagonist. The ending is unsatisfying if the audience doesn't get the payoff of seeing the protagonist respond to the invisible phere gorilla. Even if another character functions as a proxy for the protagonist in part of the story, the protagonist must return to act in the climax. In *The Hound of the Baskervilles*, Watson is the man of action who does much of the fieldwork for Holmes. Watson investigates the first part of the case alone, but Holmes returns at the global turning point because he, as the protagonist, must wrestle with the crisis and enact the climax.

Some climaxes are passive, but these cases must still abide by this rule. The protagonist may fail to act in the climax, but the action or lack of action must result from protagonist's choice. If they choose to remain passive, it needs to be intentional, not because someone else acted first and stole the protagonist's moment.

Simple Execution

As you write the climax of your story, keep in mind that it must be a unit of story at whatever level is appropriate. The climax of a scene is a beat while the climax of a global story is a scene. As a unit of story, the climax must follow the universal patterns of Story. It must contain change and it must be unexpected.

In *The Wonderful Wizard of Oz*, Dorothy decides to go to Glinda for help getting home. When she makes it to Glinda, however, her plan doesn't work out as she hoped. Glinda agrees to help, but only if Dorothy surrenders the magic cap, enslaving the flying monkeys. This unexpected turn complicates the climax.

Sometimes, climaxes are overly simplistic. The character just executes the plan. Even the most high-energy action scene will be boring and predictable if nothing unexpected happens. To keep the reader engaged, complicate the crisis. Build in unexpected moments, obstacles, and affordances to challenge your protagonist as they enact their climactic decision.

When you create an effective climax, the

reader experiences an exciting moment that satisfies their expectations for the story. It also pays off their investment in the protagonist by revealing the truth of the protagonist's character.

ANALYZING THE CLIMAX

The following questions will help you to determine whether the climax of your story or the story example you're studying effectively illustrates the choice the protagonist makes.

- **Does the protagonist of the unit of story make the choice?** Ensure the protagonist of the unit of story is making the choice. This should be the same character that faced the crisis choice.
- **Is it complicated in some way?** Explain the complications that occurred while the protagonist enacted the climax decision. The climax should be a full unit of story.
- **What does it reveal about the protagonist's character?** Describe how the climax illuminates the protagonist's character by reviewing the alternative options the protagonist did not choose. Look at

how the climax reveals the protagonist's priorities and how they value different costs and benefits.

The climax is an exciting moment that allows the reader to see the protagonist enacting the decision they make as a result of the crisis. It is also a chance for the reader to evaluate whether the protagonist made the choice they would have made in the same situation.

By actualizing one of the options that are available to the protagonist to solve the problem presented by the inciting incident, the climax narrows the possible choices down to one. This realized option is the one the story will evaluate in the controlling idea.

Once the protagonist chooses their course of action and carries it out in the climax, the next step is to explore the consequences of the protagonist's choice in the final commandment, the resolution.

7

COMMANDMENT FIVE: THE RESOLUTION

The resolution is the payoff of the decision that the protagonist makes in the climax. In this commandment, the protagonist reaps the reward or suffers the consequences of their choices. These consequences illustrate whether the choice was a good or a bad one in the arena of the story by showing how it works out for the protagonist.

This is the return on the investment the reader has made in empathizing with the protagonist and accompanying them on the journey to pursue their objects of desire. The reader has weighed the options along with the protagonist and witnessed the resulting choice. Now, they see whether the choice the protagonist made pays off in the end.

DEFINING THE RESOLUTION

The resolution illustrates the payoff of the climactic choice. It shows the outcome of the protagonist's action. This situates the entire story and defines the lasting impact the narrative will have on the reader.

In *Pride and Prejudice*, the final chapters give the reader an account of Darcy and Elizabeth's engagement and a glimpse of their married life. It shows that the problems they've faced in the story still exist—Elizabeth's family is prejudiced and Darcy's is prideful—but their love triumphs nonetheless. This positive ending elevates the Darcys to become symbols of true love. During the resolution, the reader integrates the meaning of the relationship into their own worldview.

The climax shows the decision the protagonist makes, but the reader still needs to reflect on what that action means in the context of the story. They must process the message of the narrative. The resolution gives the reader closure and allows time to consider the impact of the climactic moment. To accomplish this, it's important to give the resolution the space required for the reader to work through the meaning of the climactic decision and its consequences.

BUILDING THE RESOLUTION

Your resolution should provide a satisfying payoff to the unit of story. As you decide how to create your resolution, consider its valence and consistency with the setup.

Valence

The valence of the resolution shows whether the climactic decision worked out well for the protagonist or not. The resolution signals whether the story is prescriptive or cautionary.

A **prescriptive** story has a resolution that pays off positively for the protagonist. In this kind of resolution, the protagonist is rewarded for the climactic decision. This signals to the reader that, in the context of the story, the protagonist made the right decision. The value at stake in the story ends up in the positive. For example, Darcy and Elizabeth's happily ever after means that love triumphs, so *Pride and Prejudice* is a prescriptive story. Dorothy gets to go home, making *The Wonderful Wizard of Oz* prescriptive, too. When the reader experiences a prescriptive story and sees the positive resolution, they learn that the protagonist's climactic action is an effective strategy for achieving the objects of desire at stake in the global genre.

On the other hand, a **cautionary** story has a negative resolution. The protagonist's action fails to accomplish the intended outcome, and the global value is negative at the end of the story. For example, at the end of *The Picture of Dorian Gray*, Dorian's obsession with his painting kills him and destroys his legacy. This kind of story shows the reader a strategy to avoid. These stories are not as popular as prescriptive stories because the reader feels the pain of failure along with the protagonist, but they can be powerful if well-constructed.

Stories represent the complexity of reality, which means that actions often yield both positive and negative results. The mixed consequences add to the believability of the world because they mirror the complexity we see in our own interactions. Mixed resolutions also create a richer narrative by giving the reader a varied experience with a wide emotional range. The complexity in these resolutions stops the story from being too one-note. When analyzing resolutions with mixed impacts, weigh the different positive and negative outcomes to evaluate whether the resolution is, on balance, prescriptive or cautionary.

Consistency

The resolution must illustrate the payoff of the protagonist's choices—in particular, the climactic decision. It wraps up the unit of story by showing how it works out for the protagonist. This is where the stakes of the crisis choice and climactic decision are realized.

To keep the reader engaged and ensure that you build a realistic, believable story, the consequences of the climactic action dramatized in the resolution must be consistent with the stakes set up in the rest of the story. Review the crisis and identify the risk the protagonist assumed in choosing their path in the climax. Remember that all options in the crisis come with a tradeoff. In choosing one (or finding another option) the protagonist needs to sacrifice something, whether that means accepting the cost of a best bad choice option or forgoing the benefit of the unrealized options in an irreconcilable goods crisis. Ensure that the consequences outlined in the crisis stakes are incorporated into the resolution.

The resolution of *The Hound of the Baskervilles* is a good example of dramatizing the effect of the crisis in the resolution. In the crisis, Holmes must choose between sending

Sir Henry out of Dartmoor and trying to draw out the murderer using Sir Henry as bait. If he sends Sir Henry away, he risks alerting the murderer and allowing him to escape. If he tries to draw him out, he risks his friend's life. In the climax, he draws out the murderer, Stapleton. In the course of the climax, the stakes of both crisis options are realized. The hound attacks Sir Henry, who is left shaken and has to take a trip to recover. Stapleton escapes and only the chaos of the moor keeps him from getting away. Stapleton dies and will do no more harm, but it comes at a cost.

Following through on the stakes outlined in the crisis respects the investment the reader has made in caring about the protagonist's decision. If the climactic decision doesn't lead to the realization of the risk that the protagonist assumes in the climax (or at least nod to it), the resolution undermines the crisis. If the stakes weren't real, the protagonist's decision didn't matter, and the reader will feel cheated. Make sure to honor the attention and engagement of the reader by maintaining consistency with the stakes they care about.

ANALYZING THE RESOLUTION

When you analyze the resolution in your draft or a story example, use these questions to determine the overall valence of the resolution and ensure it resonates with the reader by maintaining consistency with the stakes of the crisis.

- **Prescriptive or Cautionary?**
  Identify whether the resolution is positive or negative. How did the climactic choice work out for the protagonist? If there were mixed results, determine whether the resolution was, on balance, positive or negative.
- **How does it pay off the Crisis?**
  Review the options and stakes you outlined when analyzing the crisis. Determine which option the protagonist chose. Go over the stakes for the options. Explain how the stakes that were outlined in the crisis apply in the resolution. Ensure the end of the story follows through on the tradeoffs that arose in the crisis.

A resolution that makes a statement about whether the climactic choice was right or wrong takes a stand on how best to achieve the objects of desire in the story. If it also pays off the crisis by staying consistent with the costs, benefits, and risks of the options the protagonist faced, it creates a strong message about the controlling idea of the story. It illustrates whether the protagonist's choice in the climax will achieve the objects of desire or not—and at what cost.

Now that we've explored how to create each commandment in a way that is effective in the narrative and suits the specific story, let's look at how the Five Commandments of Storytelling connect into a logical sequence of events that delivers the story's message to the audience.

8

BRINGING IT ALL TOGETHER

It's important to take a step back and look at how the Five Commandments work together to convey a clear controlling idea. If we don't consider the Five Commandments as a unit, we can fall into the trap of creating five independent events that don't relate to each other. This means the story won't function as a whole. When we integrate the Five Commandments into a cohesive arc, we create a compelling story that effectively communicates the controlling idea we want to convey to the audience.

To see how the Five Commandments function together, we'll look at how they complement each other to create an arc between the commandments and how they create links between different levels of the story to weave the narrative together into a coherent whole.

LINKING COMMANDMENTS

The Five Commandments of Storytelling are not just a checklist. If you build five unrelated events, they might function independently in the story, but they won't integrate the unit of story into a whole.

When you construct your Five Commandments, keep in mind not only the individual events, but also how they work together to form a cohesive arc and develop your characters.

The Arc of the Commandments

The Five Commandments of each unit of story work together as a logical, cause-and-effect sequence that binds the unit together as a whole. The inciting incident knocks your protagonist's life off balance. Because the protagonist is a simulation of a human being, the avatar reacts as a person would react, rejecting the need to change and trying to return to the status quo as soon as possible. In a world where the invisible phere gorilla is in play, the protagonist's initial worldview is not adaptive. It prevents the protagonist from observing what they need to see to have attuned responses to the arena. Because they operate under a maladaptive cognitive frame, the tactics generated by the initial strategy fail in the progressive complications until, finally, the protagonist realizes the initial strategy is not working. This is the turning point. Faced with this information, the protagonist must make a choice. At the core, they decide whether to change and adapt to the new arena or double down on the existing frame. The protagonist must then enact one of these options in the climax. The resolution shows the response from the arena, which signals whether the protagonist made the right choice.

When the Five Commandments work together in this way, they deliver the controlling idea to the reader.

Let's take a look at how the Five Commandments communicate the controlling idea of *It's a Wonderful Life*. The message of the film is: Meaning is found in sacrificing for those you love.

In the inciting incident, George Bailey's father dies and leaves him in charge of the Building and Loan. This sets up the scope of the inciting incident by posing the story-level question: Can George live a meaningful life in Bedford Falls, running the Building and Loan, or will he resent how his life has turned out?

George continues to run the business, but he hangs on to his dreams of escape from Bedford Falls. At the turning point, Uncle Billy loses a large sum of money. This puts George in danger of arrest and gives Mr. Potter the opening he needs to shut down the Building and Loan. George is now faced with losing his freedom at a much larger scale.

In the crisis, Potter tells George that he is worth more dead than alive. This moment narrows the options George can see to a choice between his life and the future of the Building and Loan. When he wishes he had never been born, his guardian angel, Clarence, shows him this alternate reality to illustrate the stakes of his choice.

In the climax, George realizes how much his life in Bedford Falls means, and he begs Clarence to allow him to return. He has seen the impact he has on his family and the community, and he chooses their happiness over his own freedom. This sacrifice is the action we will evaluate in the controlling idea.

George returns home in the resolution to face the waiting police, but his wife, Mary, brings the community together to save him from arrest. The town repays him for his loyalty and sacrifice. This establishes the story as a prescriptive tale, so it ends with the value of *Meaning*.

The clarity of the message in these Five Commandments allows the controlling idea of the story to shine through to the audience, and it has enchanted generations.

As you write your own stories, watch out for the most common issues with connection between the Five Commandments:

- The inciting incident does not tie to the climax. The inciting incident must promise the climactic action. In turn, the climax must mirror the inciting incident to show how the protagonist has changed.
- The inciting incident is unresolved at the end of the story. Stories are about processing unexpected change, so if the inciting incident is unresolved, the protagonist has failed to metabolize the invisible phere gorilla.
- The turning point does not complicate from the inciting incident. The turning point illustrates the failure of the protagonist's initial strategy, so it should arise naturally from a series of complications caused by the gradual breakdown of the procedures the protagonist relies on. A drop-in of an unexpected event undermines this dynamic,

even if it prevents the protagonist from following the initial strategy.

- The link between the turning point and the ensuing crisis decision is weak. The crisis must come directly from the turning point. Ensure the turning point is strong enough to force the protagonist to decide, and the options available in the crisis come from the turning point.
- The turning point, crisis, and climax do not follow a consistent protagonist. Switching protagonists breaks the arc and interrupts the construction of the controlling idea. Ensure the same character facing the turning point and grappling with the crisis is the one enacting the climax.
- The resolution does not tie back to the stakes established in the crisis. The crisis makes it clear that the protagonist must suffer some consequence. If they enact the climax and everything goes well, with no cost, this breaks the connection between the resolution and the crisis, undermining the controlling idea by invalidating the stakes.

When you create a unit of story with strong connections between the Five Commandments, you can communicate your controlling idea to the reader clearly and effectively.

The Role of the Protagonist

The Five Commandments of Storytelling engage the reader by creating an empathetic bond between the reader and the protagonist. To accomplish this goal, it is critical that the reader can identify the protagonist and that the protagonist plays the correct role as the Five Commandments unfold.

The inciting incident identifies the protagonist by creating empathy between the reader and an avatar. This happens when the reader witnesses the protagonist in pursuit of the objects of desire. After the inciting incident, the protagonist is locked in, and the avatar must retain this role throughout the Five Commandments.

The inciting incident is external to the protagonist because it is an invisible phere gorilla that comes into the avatar's life. The turning point is another external commandment. This response to the protagonist's actions from the arena or another avatar renders their initial strategy useless. The crisis belongs to the protagonist. It may be dramatized externally, but the question and stakes are personal. The climax also belongs to the protagonist, who must enact the climactic action. Finally, the resolution may affect the protagonist, other avatars, or the arena.

A unit of story within a larger story, like a scene inside of a global story, does not need to have the same protagonist as the broader story. However, the Five Commandments of the global story or quadrant must have a consistent protagonist. To illustrate how the protagonist changes over the course of the story, it is important that they play the correct role in all of the Five Commandments.

LINKING UNITS OF STORY

The Five Commandments of Storytelling also bind the units of story at each level into one global story that functions as a whole. When you use the Five Commandments to unite your story, you will create more than just a series of isolated episodes. The scenes work together to form sequences, acts, and the global story.

You can see this connection at work by looking at how inciting incidents weave the layers of Story together. One inciting incident can have multiple levels of promise. For example, when George Bailey's father dies, multiple questions arise. How will George react to his father's death? This is the scene-level inciting incident. Will George stay in Bedford Falls or leave on his trip as planned? This is the quadrant-level inciting incident. Will George find meaning through the work he can do for the community as the head of the Building and Loan, or will he resent having to stay in Bedford Falls? This is the story-level inciting incident. By making multiple promises, inciting incidents connect the layers of your story to make it feel like an integrated whole rather than a series of disconnected episodes.

The Five Commandments connect all of the levels of Story together, and they share common qualities across the different levels. However, the Five Commandments of each level have unique considerations depending on the unit of story in which they function.

Scene

In a scene, the Five Commandments operate at a micro level. In general, they are smaller in scale than the Five Commandments of larger units of story.

There are also scene-level considerations for inciting incidents and resolutions. These commandments are usually present within the scene, but the scene is more likely than larger units of story to happen *in medias res*, meaning the inciting incident happens off-page before the scene begins.

Resolutions must be present, but at the scene level they may be delayed and dramatized in a later scene. Use this technique sparingly, but it can boost narrative drive by creating a setup that promises the payoff of the later revelation of the resolution.

Quadrants

Each quadrant of the story contains the Five Commandments of Storytelling. These twenty moments form the skeletal scenes of the story. They are the obligatory moments of the global genre, and they work to construct effective quadrants that contribute to the global story arc.

Global

At the global level, the Five Commandments are constrained by the genre. The overall value shift must operate on the spectrum of the genre's core value. The obligatory moments of the genre define the expression of each commandment. For example, the inciting incident of a Crime story must be a crime. The genre sets limits on which events will work for each commandment.

Now that you understand how each commandment works on its own, with the other commandments, and across units of story, you can apply them in your own writing and in your study of masterworks or story examples that you want to use as patterns for your own writing. The best way to strengthen new skills is to put them into practice.

9

CONTINUING PRACTICE

We've explored the theory of the Five Commandments of Storytelling and looked at concrete examples. However, learning this information is just the first step to understanding the Five Commandments and incorporating them into your work.

To build these skills, it is critical to practice identifying and using the Five Commandments. Both writing and analysis are important components of a well-rounded practice. To learn more about establishing an effective practice, check out *The Writer's Daily Practice*. It outlines a strategy for leveling up your skills day by day.

Let's take a look at how to integrate the Five Commandments of Storytelling into your daily practice. In your writing, you can use them to plan a scene or your global story. When you analyze a story example, you can focus on each scene and break down the Five Commandments. You can also fill out a foolscap to explore the global story, which requires identifying the Five Commandments of each quadrant.

PLAN A SCENE

Scenes are the building blocks of stories. If you focus your practice on learning to write better scenes, you'll write better stories.

When using the Five Commandments of Storytelling to plan a scene, it's not always helpful to address them in order. Experiment to find the process that works for you. This is how I plan a scene using the Five Commandments.

First, think about the purpose of the scene. Each story unit moves the story from Point A to Point B in terms of value. How is this scene going to shift? How will it change the trajectory of the global value?

Next go to the climax. What action will your character take in the scene? This action should accomplish the change you identified.

Now that you know what the character is going to do, work on building the crisis. What is the cost of that action? What alternative courses of action could they have taken? These components form the crisis tradeoff.

The turning point gives rise to the crisis question. What event will make the choices in the crisis plausible? Make sure your turning point is directly related to the crisis, so it makes the possible choices reasonable ones. This ensures that it's a real choice.

Next, decide on the resolution. How does this chain of turning point, crisis, and climax work out? What consequences result from the tradeoffs the character made?

Finally, create the inciting incident. Don't overthink this at the scene level. It can be simple—just a situation that brings the characters together. They might go out for coffee, throw a party, or land a job interview. Get your protagonist into a space where story events can unfold. This is realistic because most of the time we don't show up expecting a story to happen. Instead, your protagonist is living a normal life until the invisible phere gorilla drops in.

PLAN A STORY

When you plan a story, you can follow the same procedure outlined above to plan a scene. To figure out the shift in value, pick a global genre. The core value at stake is specific to your genre. This choice also gives you guidelines for your climax, which must be the core event for the genre. You can learn more about each genre's core value and core event in *The Four Core Framework* by Shawn Coyne. Use the Five Commandments to create genre-specific events that you can use as an outline for the arc of your global story.

ANALYZE A SCENE

When analyzing a scene example, you can use the Five Commandments to identify the change in the scene. Practice applying the lessons you've learned in this book to identify the Commandments of the scene. You can also use the Five Commandments to determine and describe the story event. The chain of events in the turning point, crisis, and climax will help you to find the value shift at play in the scene. The climax shows the protagonist's tactic to enact the shift. The resolution gives you the impact on the story. Taken together, these steps will help you craft a story event that summarizes the change in the scene.

ANALYZE A STORY

The Five Commandments of Storytelling are integrated into the Story Grid Global Foolscap analysis. To fill out your foolscap, identify the Five Commandments in each quadrant of the story. This will help you understand the movement of the story at the global level.

When you analyze your favorite stories using the Five Commandments, you will observe masterful constructions of each commandment and how they work together to form compelling stories. You'll learn about the nuances of how each commandment functions within a story. Then, take those learnings and apply them in your writing practices. Over time, you will build the skill of creating strong and effective story arcs that will engage your readers and communicate your message to them across space and time.

10

CONCLUSION

Every writer wants to communicate with readers and make a lasting impact.

Now, you can build the skills to do that by using the Five Commandments of Storytelling to craft a story that functions as a coherent whole and conveys a meaningful controlling idea to your reader. This is what changes minds, touches hearts, and affects lives. You have a wonderful power as a storyteller.

With your new understanding of the Five Commandments of Storytelling, you can create better stories. Continue to hone your skills by studying masterworks and practicing the application of these skills in your writing.

The Five Commandments of Storytelling are the keys to sending your message to your audience. What you have to say matters. Keep practicing your craft because the world needs your story.

ABOUT THE AUTHOR

DANIELLE KIOWSKI is a Story Grid Certified Editor based in Las Vegas, Nevada. She grew up with her nose in a book and loves a good story, especially if it's set in a world of urban fantasy or magical realism. As an editor, Danielle is dedicated to empowering ambitious professionals to fulfill their dreams of becoming authors by supporting their development of sustainable and productive writing practices. She believes Story is a fundamental building block of the human experience, and everyone, regardless of their chosen profession, can lead a more meaningful life by engaging with narrative. You can find her online at daniellekiowski.com and writersbynight.com.

ABOUT THE EDITOR

LESLIE WATTS is a Story Grid Certified Editor, Editor-in-Chief of Story Grid Publishing, and a writer, based in Maine. Leslie has written craft-focused articles for the Fundamental Fridays blog and craft books, including *Point of View*, *Conventions and Obligatory Moments* (with Kimberly Kessler), *What's the Big Idea?* (with Shelley Sperry), and a masterwork analysis guide to Malcolm Gladwell's *The Tipping Point* (with Shelley Sperry). As an editor, Leslie helps fiction and nonfiction clients write epic stories that matter. She believes writers become better storytellers through study and practice, and editors owe a duty of care to help writers with specific and supportive guidance.

Made in the USA
Columbia, SC
13 October 2021